THE FRICK COLLEC

Anshen Transdisciplinary Lectureships in Art, Science and the Philosophy of Culture

---

MONOGRAPH ONE

W9-ACN-353
D/RF LATAM
1-55921-072-9   E
200   2826208009953
$9.95

THE REAL DISCOVERY OF AMERICA: MEXICO NOVEMBER 8, 1519

by Hugh Thomas

MOYER BELL LIMITED

MOUNT KISCO, NEW YORK & LONDON

Published by Moyer Bell Limited

Copyright © 1992 by The Frick Collection

All rights reserved. No part of this publication may
be reproduced or transmitted in any form or by any
means electronic or mechanical, including photo-
copying, recording or any information retrieval
system, without permission in writing from Moyer
Bell Limited, Colonial Hill, Mt. Kisco, New York
10549 or 71 Great Russell Street, London WC1B
3BN.

First Edition

LIBRARY OF CONGRESS
CATALOGING-IN-PUBLICATION DATA

Thomas, Hugh, 1931–
    The real discovery of America : Mexico
November 8, 1519 / by Hugh Thomas. — 1st ed.
        p. cm.—(Anshen transdisciplinary lecture-
ships in art, science, and the philosophy of culture :
monograph 1)
    ISBN 1-55921-069-9
    1. Cortes,   Hernan,   1485–1547.   2. Mexico—
History—Conquest. 1519–1540. I. Title. II. Series.
F1230.C835T5   1992
972'.02'092—dc20   92-28133
                                                        CIP

Printed in the United States of America
Distributed in America by Rizzoli International
Publications & in Europe by Pandemic Ltd.

CONTENTS

INTRODUCTION

I am very happy to introduce, on behalf of the Trustees and the staff of The Frick Collection, the first Anshen Transdisciplinary Lecture in Art, Science and the Philosophy of Culture. It is an honor for me to do so, and a very special pleasure for us to have, as our guests, so many distinguished scholars in all aspects of the arts, sciences, and social sciences, as well as philosophy.

We are here, drawn by Ruth Anshen's magnetic power to cross the barriers which frequently exist among various disciplines and fields of inquiry. We are gathered together with our guests from a wide variety of professions, but, we trust, without any departmentalism. I am reminded on this occasion of one of Dr. Anshen's earliest mentors, Alfred North Whitehead, who wrote of an evening many years ago, when Junior Fellows had just been created at Harvard. It is reported that Whitehead said, "At these Fellows' gatherings there is no 'departmentalism.'" And he emphasized that word. "The men studying literature are at elbows with men studying biology and mathematics. In the Harvard faculty itself, I notice a good deal of departmentalism. You would think the men in one department had nothing to learn from their colleagues in another, or else that"—and the report goes that his eyes twinkled roguishly—"they were protecting themselves from contamination."

So we salute, first of all, Dr. Ruth Anshen, who is leading us out of worlds where such contamination may be suspected. She has been, for many years, a powerful, almost magical leader, who has written so much herself, and inspired so many others to write and to take up important issues in transdisciplinary ways. Our gratitude is first of all—and lastly—to Ruth Anshen.

A brief introduction to her and her work may be found in the programs which I hope you all have. There, you will also find introductions to Lord Thomas of Swynnerton, and to the leader of the discussion to follow his lecture, who is Professor Klor de Alva of Princeton.. We are deeply indebted to both of them.

Lord Thomas is justly one of the most celebrated historians. He will look with us into a rather special, unusual subject, which you will note when you hear the title, "The Real Discovery of America: Mexico, November 8, 1519."

Professor Klor de Alva was born in Mexico, knows intimately Aztec and Nahua culture, and is a distinguished anthropologist. Together with these men, we hope that many of you will join in reflecting on, and talking about, what Sir Thomas Browne hundreds of years ago realized: that before its discovery—and I quote Sir Thomas Browne—"That great antiquity *America* lay buried for thousands of years." We trust that there will be a number of you gathered here this evening, who will look across other cultures, other disciplines, to create the total experience of this first Anshen Transdisciplinary Lecture.

Therefore, with no further introduction, I should like to call on Dr. Ruth Nanda Anshen to inaugurate these lectureships.

—Charles Ryskamp

PREFACE

The Frick Collection is now extending its glorious influence as an oasis of culture to include The Anshen Transdisciplinary Lectureships in Art, Science and the Philosophy of Culture. We are all deeply indebted to Charles for his distinguished, inspiring leadership.

I would like to say a few brief words about the meaning of these transdisciplinary lectureships. All great changes are preceded by a vigorous intellectual reorganization. We hope that these transdisciplinary lectureships, not interdisciplinary which isolates them from each other, can bring about a correlation of ideas which are concerned with an effort to overcome the mutual unintelligibility among the various disciplines. We hope to create a crucible of knowledge. This may be an utopian aspiration but a map without utopia is just not worth looking at.

The notion of a mere fact is the triumph of the abstract

intellect. A single fact in isolation is the primary myth required for finite thought. There is no such fact: Connectedness, relationship is the essence of all things of all types. No fact is ever merely itself. These transdisciplinary lectureships could bring about a synthesis of those ideas concerned not only with sense data and logical universals but with the status of values and the bearing of these values on conduct. A cooperative effort to accomplish this, to exhibit where representatives of different scholarly disciplines agree or disagree, how much agreement there is and on what specific points could, hopefully, result in a condition of complementarity. It is the fragmentation of the disciplines which has rendered them comparatively ineffectual.

Such a correlation of ideas could be an antidote to the disjunction between the empirical approach and the theoretical principles, between methods of observation and speculative doctrine, between information and knowledge, between thought and feeling, between religion and theology. Transdisciplinary lectureships could become a cultural directory for the guidance of those principles valid for education, indeed for culture as well. By gathering in a transdisciplinary crucible science and the humanities the lectureships could become a laboratory for the presentation of critical problems, a collective intelligence so highly developed as to make individual disciplines no longer isolated from each other but relevant to each other, for a new power is given to the mind by science, by philosophy, by art, and includes, of course, the transcendent in relation to the concrete. These transdisciplinary lectureships could portray the inherent wisdom and the power of the human mind and its fitness above all for the nature of experience including ethics, of course, and our responsibility to our ethical conscience. And if our lectureships are right, our unitary approach can create moral and spiritual values and the issues of consciousness to guide us to a more noble path for survival than the uncertain course we presently follow.

This is a dream, but a dream which has come true and a prayer which has been answered here in this oasis of culture.

—Ruth Nanda Anshen

THE REAL DISCOVERY OF AMERICA: MEXICO, NOVEMBER 8, 1519

THE REAL DISCOVERY OF AMERICA

Dr. Anshen initially suggested that she would like me to write about some of the problems of modern democracy. Having recently completed ten years of political endeavor—now best forgotten—and having embarked again, with great satisfaction, on a life of full-time historical study, I proposed to Dr. Anshen that I might contribute instead something just as worthy of the noble cause to which the Frick Collection lectures are devoted, namely, a study of the discovery of Mexico by the Spanish in 1519; or should I say, to be fair, the discovery of the Spanish by the Mexicans?

Dr. Anshen, as you can imagine, generously agreed, and she even accepted my rather mysterious title intended to indicated that the phrase, "The Discovery of America," really is a rather pretentious way of describing exactly what happened in 1492.

I think I conceived the phrase, "The Real Discovery of

America," on one summer day; as you all know, what you think of on a summer day is something you should forget on the next day. But what I think I had in mind when I put the title like this was something rather like this: Suppose in 1492, a Mexican fleet had crossed the Atlantic, touched the Azores, looked in for a moment at Madeira, picked up some sherry and measles at the Canaries (as Columbus picked up tobacco and syphilis in Cuba); could we accept that a Mexican fleet had discovered *Europe*?

We are still allowed to assume that Columbus landed in the Bahamas, Cuba, and Santo Domingo, though it's not certain that those claims will be sustained until the end of 1992, but we must assume that for the moment. What he found in those islands, bore, I suggest to you, as little relation to the real riches of ancient America, as say, the Bahamas does now to the real riches of modern America.

You think, of course, that I am teasing you. You'll be saying, surely you can't be suggesting that there's any chance at all of a Mexican fleet having crossed the Atlantic. The Chinese, admittedly, sent a fleet to East Africa in the fifteenth century, but the Aztecs in the Canary Isles? Well, in a literal sense, of course, if you put it like that, it's a tease. The ancient Mexicans had many things, but had neither the astrolabe nor the compass, nor the great sails of the great galleons which were essential for crossing the Atlantic. They had canoes for fishing, for transport in the lakes of Mexico or on off-shore voyages, but there is no more chance of a Mexican fleet crossing the Atlantic in 1492, than of a Spanish fleet crossing the Atlantic in 1392.

And that comment, to some extent, places the degree of

development of Spain and ancient Mexico in proper maritime perspective. For, of course, the great inventions which made possible the discovery of America, the conquests in America, were all fifteenth century inventions. And there was really no chance at all of a Spanish fleet crossing the Atlantic in 1392.

In most respects, of course, taking things in general, Europe was technologically immensely superior to Mexico in 1519—perhaps in other ways, though we shall come to that. But what surely should strike us most about that meeting between the ancient Americans and the Spanish of the Renaissance, that meeting which occurred in November, 1519, that meeting between Cortes and Montezuma, on that still identifiable, magical spot on the causeway leading to Mexico, Tenochtitlan, that meeting, which was, in fact, the real discovery of America—what strikes us surely most—or what strikes us most about that meeting is not the great differences, technological or other in the levels of attainment between the two societies, but rather the curious similarities between two societies, which had not previously been in any connection with each other; similarities which would lead at the time the explosive physician, Paracelsus, to argue that God must have carried out two creations: one in the West and one in the East; similarities which have persuaded some quite reasonable people that someone from Europe or from India—St. Thomas, or perhaps, even think of it, St. Brendan—might just have been there before and planted, among other things, the cult of crosses, which were found by the Spanish in Yucatan; similarities which could even suggest that—or might even suggest to us now—that there are certain innate dispositions, dispositions of Homo sapiens, toward certain manifestations. For though the ancestors of the ancient Mexicans, like all early Americans, came originally from Asia, the date of their crossing was not only before the opening of the Bering Straits, but centuries before the establishment of settled societies in Asia. Consider just a few of the similarities between Europe and the Aztecs at random. (I use that phrase Aztecs as a synonym for the Mexicans, knowing that it is perhaps not quite proper to do so.)

First of all, the Aztecs worshipped a variety of gods connected with agriculture or natural phenomenon, rain, the moon, harvesting, sowing, and, of course, the sun. So, of course, did most of the Old World for many centuries before the coming of the great transnational universal religions. Here, perhaps, the Mexicans may have been in reach in the early fifteenth century of the same sort of development as occurred in the Old World. People read and appreciate the poetry of the poet king of Texcoco, Nezahulacoyotl, but the remarkable character of his work, seems to me, are not the poems, interesting as they undoubtedly are, but the prayers interspersed as they are in most collections. The prayers to, for example, the supreme giver, or the single god who, perhaps but not certainly, could have been an antecedent to a Mexican cult of just such a universal religion with a single deity, and with an abandonment of the nature gods, which I've mentioned. Some of the details of other Mexican practices, such as plunging a new-born child into water before he was named, are startlingly familiar to Christians.

The political structure of ancient Mexico does not have

an exact equivalent, I agree, in the Old World, but, nevertheless, there are enough similarities to make one realize one is dealing with a political society which is familiar. For example, Mexico, as found by Cortés, has an emperor sitting in the capital. Through military conquest he received tribute from about three hundred and fifty subject cities, "a mosaic of cities," as Jacques Soustelle put it. Though there is not exact equivalent, there are plenty of places with some similarities to what went on in Mexico, from, for example, the Tartar empire; also, quite differently, but in a different way comparable, that society of prosperous, well-ordered republics, loosely federated together under a titular monarch, which was the chief character of the lowlands of the Netherlands, when Charles the Fifth came to the throne in 1519, the throne of the Empire.

The rulers of Mexico were, like many European monarches in theory elected by the tribe as a whole, but, as often happened, and, in fact, as usually happened in the Old World and would happen very soon with the electors to Spanish municipal councils in Mexico itself, the College of Electors become increasingly small and was eventually confined to a few grandees. As began to occur in the Holy Roman Empire under the Hapsburgs, the Aztec royal family, the imperial title in the Aztec world, was confined to a single royal family.

Mexico had a strong sense of the importance and the implications of law. They had professional judges, and, as was soon shown after the conquest transculturally, if not transdisciplinarily, they shared a capacity to adapt their customs to the practices of Spain, the Spaniards, of course, were themselves highly legally-minded then as now. This was shown, for example, when the citizens of the city of Coyoacan, then just outside Mexico, sued the descendants of Cortés in the 1560s for compensation for Cortés's seizure of the old chief's house in Coyoacan to live in just after the conquest. The Mexicans were supposed to be monogamous, but the ruler was committed to have many women. Equally, Cortés's Christians were called on to have only one wife, but there were occasions, dare I say so, when Cortés and other Christian leaders in Mexico did not keep that rule very precisely.

Treatment of women did not differ very much in the Old World from what happened in Mexico. Generally subordinate in 1500, women occasionally, through the accident of birth, might come to a position of outstanding importance, but that was extremely rare.

The inclusion every year of a tribute of "twenty-five thousand handfuls of birds' feathers," which had to be paid by the people of Socunusco to the Imperial Mexico, shows the Old America was as environmentally negligent as was Old Europe. Military prowess was probably prized more in Mexico than it was in contemporary Europe. The practice of preparing male children for the professional arms from birth has a very strong echo of Sparta, or even Prussia. The Mexican hieroglyph for government makes clear the military role in the states since it consisted of a bow and arrows, a shield, and a throwing stone. No Western society that I know went so far in relation to a military society as prescribing the burying of the umbilical cords of male children at the gates of the city whence an enemy might come.

Of course, Mexico lacked many things which gave Europe in the sixteenth century its special quality: the use of iron, beasts of burden, writing, of course, and reading, though, in this last instance, reading had only just recently been made easy or accessible to the multitude through printing. I would doubt very much if more than a small minority of Cortés's expedition were, in fact, able to read. This lack of sophisticated writing in Mexico, to some extent, was compensated for by the use of ideograms and hieroglyphs. Perhaps that method of communication could, in a short time—or perhaps a long time—have matured. After all, the Mayan superior script was still in use in Yucatan in the 1520s when the Spanish arrived.

All the same, that was not the same thing as reading and writing. This reliance on primitive methods of communication may just have affected Mexicans' inability to distinguish myth from reality, though, at that time, that line was not always very firmly drawn in Spain either. Cortés and his co-conquistadors were, after all, men born about 1480. They were—if they could read, that is—men of the first generation of readers of the printed word, and they were the first generation of young men who knew that the printed book could be a source of pleasure. That did not mean that they always read Erasmus or Cicero. On the contrary, their appetite very often was for chivalresque novels of the type which, later on, Cervantes would mock in Don Quixote. That reading, in turn, lead to many fantasies. For example, Cortés's lieutenant, Sandoval, not otherwise a man of dreams, was always thinking that behind the next headland there would surely be that marvelous island, California, where the Amazon queen, Califia, would be found ruling her marvelous Amazons, independent of male intervention. Cortés too, in his instructions from the Governor of Cuba, was told specifically to find out if, in Yucatan, there were men with the heads of dogs.

Both the Spanish and the Mexicans put faith not only in their established orthodox religions but in omens. Both had admiration for courage in adversity. The Mexicans were fond of proverbs; so were the Spanish.

Two reactions are likely, I suppose, to this comparison, which, in a transdisciplinary manner, I've been making between the customs and the attitudes of the peoples of ancient Mexico and our European ancestors. On the one hand, is the dark side of Old Mexico. I should have mentioned the pantheon of monstrous gods and the childish legends, not to speak of that long line of victims, chiefly prisoners of war or slaves, who—year in, year out—were dragged up, or went willingly up, the steps of the pyramids to have their hearts torn out to be offered to a supposedly hungry Sun, while their bodies were later ceremonially eaten (or as Professor Harmer improbably suggested fifteen years ago, just eaten for pleasure). Human sacrifice was certainly on the increase in Mexico when the Spanish got there. The figures in the chronicles of, for example, Father Duran, must well be exaggerated. All the same, there was no precedent for the number of those offered to the Sun on the occasion of the dedication of the great new temple of Mexico City, or Mexico, in 1487.

Yet it is fair to say that there were some qualifying

circumstances. For example, those royal visitors who came from other cities, both tributary and independent of the Mexican empire, to that very same ritual of the dedication of the new temple, were shocked by the scale of what was going on, as those same chronicles record. Is it not fair to say that shock recalled in tranquility often is the principle cause of revolutionary change?

Secondly, those who held out most effectively against the Mexican empire before the arrival of the Spanish, the Tarascans to the north in what is now Michocan, had a much lower lend of human sacrifice. Thirdly, and very importantly, the equivocal but very important god, Quetzacoatl, whose alleged role in explaining Mexico's subordination to Cortes continues to be controversial. Quetzacoatl was an enemy of sacrifice. Who knows what the future of human sacrifice would have been if the Mexicans had not been invaded in 1519?

Perhaps, though, there is another point. Perhaps if Montezuma really thought that Cortes was a reincarnation of Quetzacoatl, his chief anxiety was less that the god might really come up to Mexico and not only abolish human sacrifice, but punish the sacrificers, of whom Montezuma, ex-high-priest as well as emperor, was likely to be an outstanding candidate. As a matter of fact, Cortes did precisely all that, so that if Montezuma really thought that Cortes was Quetzacoatl, that particular anxiety was quite well based.

But it is fair to remember, when thinking of that dark side of Mexico, that Europe too had its unhappy passages, to put it in a very modest way. In battle, for example, the Mexicans fought to capture prisoners of war for sacrifice, this being their chief strategic undoing. The Europeans usually fought to kill; prisoners were an embarrassment. Nor were the Spanish morally in a strong position to complain in relation to human sacrifice, when—this is an old debating point, but the one thing I learnt from exposure to politics, is that repetition is the essence of political life—when one considers the Jews, the Muslims, expelled, imprisoned, or burned in the forty years between the establishment of the Inquisition and Cortés's entry into Tenochtitlan. True, human sacrifice differed from what was done by the Spanish in Spain and elsewhere, since it was an essential part of Mexican religion.

I may have critics in my arguments from another angle: those who would reproach me for neglecting to emphasize ways in which the ancient Mexicans were the equal of, even the superiors to, the Western Europeans of the sixteenth century. We are thinking, after all, of people whose achievements in weaving and in pottery were certainly equivalent to their European contemporaries, and whose goldsmithery, and feathercraft, in some respects, and certainly mathematics, were perhaps superior. The Aztecs knew how to polish stone so that it shone beautifully. It is not easy to make judgments of superiority or inferiority in respect to art in the best of times. It is particularly difficult where the Aztec featherwork and gold are concerned, since most of the finest products are lost. The Spanish wanted Aztec gold melted down in bars for use as currency or for the embellishment of churches in Spain itself. Hence the shortage in our great museums of gold artifacts from Mexico. Even the visitor to the Frick Collection cannot recapture the enthusiasm of Dürer, when, in August 1520, he saw an exhibition, in the Hotel de Ville in Brussels, of the great treasures of Mexico.

As for mathematics, the ancient Mexicans could count in as sophisticated a way as the Europeans, and their calendars were more accurate than ours. Figures, perhaps, are more important than letters for the efficient management of society. That the Aztecs were efficient is obvious, considering even our modern preoccupations. The Mexicans were in some ways at a higher level than the Europeans. We are all interested in universal education. The Aztecs had it. We are interested and concerned by the rate of crime; the Aztecs kept it to a low level, because—at least so the chroniclers thought—of the severe punishments, of which a typical measure was that if a crime were committed by a particular village, the elders of the place were required to deliver the culprit, or else they would suffer themselves the punishment proscribed.

In good manners, I dare say the Mexicans were then, as now, the superior to most of those with whom they came into contact. "As courteous as a Mexican Indian," was a Spanish saying as early as 1550.

The quality of Mexican culture was observed at the time. "One does not need witnesses from heaven," wrote the great Bishop Las Casas, "to demonstrate that these were political peoples with towns, inhabited places of large size, villas, and cities." Cortés in a dispatch wrote to Charles V: "The natives of these parts are of much greater intelligence that those of the Caribbean Islands. They appear to us to possess such understanding and reason as to be each one of them generally capable of order and harmony."

But if the Mexicans were as I have described, how was it then that so small a number of Spaniards, a thousand at most, far from home in an unfamiliar and difficult climate, were able to defeat them, particularly, since the work of the California school of history—Professors Simpson, Borah, and Cook—long-ago established from the examination of tribute roles that the population was high; though whether it was as high as they thought seems improbable.

To explain this is not quite so easy as it often seems. Perhaps we should look on Cortés and his conquistadors as a band of foreign-financed terrorists, such as have caused havoc in a dozen countries out of all proportion to their numbers. But there are other political explanations. The Spanish were clever enough to realize that the subject nations of the Mexican empire had so deep a hatred of the imperial power that they were willing to serve as the sepoys to Cortés and his army. Hence, a modern Mexican writer was able to write: "Mexico was conquered by the Indians, just as Mexican independence was won by the Spanish." Yet another explanation is, of course, technological. Spanish steel swords, Spanish cannons, sailing ships, horses, dogs, certainly indicated the superiority of European technology. I say European because Cortés's expedition had Italians, Portuguese, and Greeks within its ranks. Yet, we've learned to be suspicious of theories of history which attribute to technological innovations alone the reasons for the changes in history, in battles as in agriculture.

Having mentioned the similarities between the great indigenous societies of the Americas and the Spanish, this brings me to the difference, and the differences were the things that counted. The first and most important was that the Spanish were curious about their surroundings. Time after time, the documents describe conquistadors being asked to find out the secret of this or that territory. We should compare that curiosity, that interest in knowing what was going on to the evident lack of interest of the Aztecs in what was happening beyond their frontiers. There was contact between Cuba and Yucatan before the Spanish reached Yucatan, but it was on a very small scale and probably accidental. And certainly the Mexicans seemed to have little knowledge of what the Spanish were doing in the Caribbean before they reached their own country. They certainly didn't know that, in effect, the Spanish had been conducting labor camps in the whole of the Caribbean for twenty-five years before 1519.

The second great difference is that the Spanish were capable of, even relished, discussion about the nature of their imperial endeavors. Spain of the early sixteenth century, for all of the brutalities and iniquities which I have perhaps overstressed, were thoughtful and argumentative. Ideas counted. Cardinal Cisneros was already achieving, early in the sixteenth century, the beginning of the transformation of the Spanish church, which foreshadowed the Counter-Reformation. Erasmus had his great intellectual conquests in Spain just before the Spanish conquered Mexico.

So far as the empire was concerned, the Dominican Order were in the forefront of a prolonged debate to insist that since the natives of the New World were plainly human beings they as plainly had souls and, therefore, could be saved. By what right, they asked, could they, therefore, be subject into slavery? The Dominicans also asked by what right did the conquistadors invade other lands? For two generations, arguments along these lines raged throughout Spain, in the Court, in universities, in monasteries, and in discussions elsewhere, arguments as to whether the Mexicans and the other Indians of the New World were, in fact, as Aristotle had put it in relation to the Persians—Aristotle had recently been translated and even more recently printed—whether the Mexicans and the other Indians of the New World were, in fact, slaves by nature.

The complaints of the opponents of the Dominicans and those who sustained the arguments that the Indians of the New World were slaves by nature, read curiously now, but they should not be wholly dismissed without consideration. Thus, when presented by Bishop de Las Casas or Cortés with arguments that, for example, the gold and silver objects so admired by Dürer, put Mexico on a different level from the people of the Caribbean, Ginés de Sepúlveda, a formidable conservative polemicist, caused one of his characters to insist, in a dialogue printed in 1540 or so, that spiders and bees and other such species, which even the Dominicans would not insist had a soul, could create great works of art in the shape of webs and hives; so the production of beauty was not necessarily a sign of grace.

Also, this character, to whom Sepúlveda gave the name Democrates, insisted that the chief mark of Old Mexico was that nobody did anything on their own, being wholly subordinate and wholly at the disposal of the king. This submissiveness, he argued, did not derive from force but was involuntary and spontaneous, a sure sign of a servile attitude. How can we doubt, Sepúlveda then had Democrates say, that these unlettered people have been justly conquered by Charles V? Incidentally, one of the first reports about Mexico, in one of the first-ever newspapers, the *Neuwe Zeitung* of Nuremberg in 1520, complained more or less in the same terms, that the people of Mexico are so obedient that, if the king tells them to go into the forest and die, they do it. Alas, as we all know, Nuremberg's own experience of excessive servility was to be delayed five hundred years.

It seems essential to emphasize that the discussion about the intellectual basis for the empire, which no other imperial power embarked upon, paradoxically was one reason why the Spanish had the intellectual will, as well as the military strength, to consolidate its conquests.

My chief arguments are that there are more things in common between ancient America (Mexico) and Old Europe than most people suppose. Secondly, that the fact that the Mexicans before Cortes has kings, noblemen, priests, judges, poets, generals, money, commerce, classes, taxes, and laws, among other things, suggests that these things may be not a thing characteristic of the old honor but embedded in human nature. Thirdly, that the difference of importance between the two peoples, the Spanish and the Mexicans, was not so much the steel of Spanish swords, nor even in such things as Cortes's equine strategy, as a learned article once described it, but the Spanish capacity to wonder, and above all, to wonder what was happening around the next corner. Their proclivity to debate, even to think, was clearly of the greatest importance.

A subsidiary argument, which I hope will be seen as an undercurrent beneath what I have said, is that a consideration of the nature of the two worlds, which came together in 1519, can only be properly appreciated by respect for the philosophical, scientific, and artistic history of the matter, as well as the political history of the transdisciplinary approach to knowledge to which our philanthropic and learned friend, Dr. Anshen, devotes her formidable and imaginative energy.

APPENDIX

DISCUSSION

J. Jorge Klor de Alva: This book is serving as a symbol and as a stimulus for the kinds of discussions and the kinds of rethinking taking place in the social sciences, taking place certainly in the area of philosophy, taking place in the arts, and elsewhere on the nature of the transformations taking place in the world today, with a reflection on the transformations that have taken place in the past. I have, on a number of occasions, identified the moment that we are living through as a second quincentennial moment, and, by way of some remarks to begin our discussion, I want to frame that in the following fashion.

Five hundred years ago, at the time that Lord Thomas is addressing, the European world entered the worlds of the indigenous peoples of the Americas, of the indigenous peoples in Southern Asia, and Africa, and elsewhere, and began a series of dramatic transformations whose initiation in the case of Central Mexico, Lord Thomas has very perceptively defined. And five hundred years later, at this moment, all of us are aware that a reversal of that first quincentennial moment is taking place. We are living through a second quincentennial moment. Now it is people from all these various areas who are moving into Europe, who are moving into the United States, into other places. And this second quincentennial moment, like the first quincentennial moment, has been extremely disturbing, extremely unsettling, and extremely transforming.

At the historical level, we are seeing a great deal of revision and rethinking what those first contacts were all about. We could certainly discuss at great length Lord Thomas's position, Lord Thomas's interpretations; but more important than debating or analyzing and looking at the specifics that are being raised by this very important lecture, is an invitation to all of us to discuss this particular phenomenon in the light of what it means symbolically to be discussing such a phenomenon by a historian from the British Isles, being commented on by a Mexican in the Frick Collection five hundred years later, and under the rubric of an analysis and a thinking through of this Anshen Transdisciplinary Lecture in Art, Science and Philosophy of Culture.

I would like to close with this observation: Not only is it five hundred years after this very transcendent event that Lord Thomas has discussed, not only is it five hundred years since then, it is the end of the twentieth century. It is the end of the century. It is the end of the millennium. It is a time when in the areas of philosophy, in the areas of history, in the areas of anthropology, certainly throughout the human sciences, and certainly in art, and perhaps we might say, even particularly in art, and in the literary field, new theoretical perspectives are coming to the fore that are having the unsettling effect of precisely breaking through disciplines whose beginnings we can, for the most part, date, but whose beginnings we might say come from the eighteenth century, arise certainly after the Renaissance, reach a certain moment of real consolidation around the eighteenth century with the Enlightenment, develop into what we call modernity. And now these disciplines, whose long histories hark back and have their roots in the Enlightenment are now being put in question. A notion, if I may add, like conquest, a notion like colonization, notions of representation, notions of the writing of history, the narrativity of history, notions about the nature of text, and ultimately notions about the nature of the subject and whether the subject itself that we take so much for granted, all of us children of the Enlightenment, put in question by all of a sudden being studied through a number of disciplines. And more important than that—and I so like the title—rather than interdisciplinary, going beyond those disciplines to put the very disciplines themselves into question.

I think that the kinds of issues that have been raised by Lord Thomas's own analysis at this historical juncture give us plenty of opportunity to discuss these very important transformations, then and today, and their significance altogether.

Paul O. Kristeller: I am not an expert on this topic, but I am an amateur traveler, museum visitor, and art historian. And I have seen many important monuments of Mexican culture of the sixteenth century and before. When I heard Lord Thomas comment on the objects admired by Dürer in Brussels, which apparently got lost, I remembered that we have equally important specimens in various European museums, especially in the Vienna Hofburg where the objects sent by Maximilian of Mexico in the nineteenth century are displayed, and, above all, in the so-called Museum of Anthropology in Mexico City, which has marvelous specimens, not only of Aztec culture, but also of all previous periods of pre-Columbian American culture. I would say they contain many objects that deserve our admiration, but I do not agree that the specimens, especially of textiles and of pottery, are superior to the textiles and pottery produced in the West, not only in the fifteenth or sixteenth century, but back from antiquity and down through the Middle Ages. The Western art works are different, but they are not inferior.

The other point is this: I know of no evidence that the mathematics of the Aztecs was superior to Western mathematics. We have no textual evidence that the Aztecs or their American predecessors had anything comparable to algebra or to the theory of equations, theories which were thoroughly developed in Europe by 1492, some of them based on Greek sources recently made available, some of them transmitted from the Greeks through the Indians and Arabs. I wonder what the evidence for the superior mathematics of the Mexicans is. I think these are the two main questions which I should like to raise. I also might have asked whether the Mexicans produce anything comparable to the literature or philosophy of the West from antiquity to the Renaissance.

DISCUSSION

*   *   *

Arthur Schlesinger, Jr.: I am much interested by Lord Thomas's argument. Professor Klor de Alva has reminded us that, as the quincentennial of Columbus impends, the view has arisen that the arrival of Columbus had a destructive effect on what is portrayed as idyllic societies in the Americas, societies where people lived in harmony with the land, and where European habits of violence and destruction brought significant changes. Of course, there are evident objections to this view. Mayan civilization, for example, many people believe, disappeared because of the exhaustion of the soil, and so on. But the whole drift of Lord Thomas's argument was to suggest the great similarities in habits of violence and destruction between Old Europe and Old America.

Of course, as Hugh Thomas reminds us, Cortes and his small body of men could never have gotten anywhere in Mexico had not the hatred of the Aztecs been so great among other Mexican tribes, that they happily joined Cortes in overthrowing the tyrant in Mexico City. We should keep all this in mind when we hold that the arrival of Europeans in America has been the root of all evil.

James H. Schwartz: I am a neuroscientist and would like to ask Lord Thomas and Professor Klor de Alva a question. Neuroscientists now tend to think of the brain as the last frontier, whose conquest is soon to come. What do you think about that? To focus the discussion with the remarks of the last commentator, neuroscientists do believe in natural law to some degree. We think that there are natural (or innate) structural and functional features of the nervous system, and we are becoming more neo-Kantian because of our biology. As a consequence, the great cultural achievements made by *both* native Americans and Europeans by 1519 do not seem surprising, since both populations were endowed with *human* brains.

On the other hand, Lord Thomas asserts that the Mexicans' lack of curiosity contributed in large part to their conquest by the Spaniards. In the early sixteenth century, this curiosity was a distinctive aspect of European culture that gave rise to science as we know it, and, in this century, may culminate in the conquest of mind and brain. Professor Klor de Alva, how do you see the relationships between curiosity (and science) and discovery (and conquest) in terms of postmodern interpretation of text, the very thing that you just mentioned? And how would you see these problems in the light of biology? More specifically, the dialectic between a Kantian structural basis of mind and critical social influences on behavior and cultural achievement?

Marvin Ruderman: I am a theoretical physicist. Hugh Thomas gave us reasons why, in the confrontation between the conquistadors and the Mexicans, a thousand Spaniards could win such a quick and decisive victory. One of the great differences, apparently, between the Europeans and the Mexicans was in their different immune systems. The American groups had been isolated for millennia. The Europeans had considerable immunity to those infectous diseases which they brought into Mexico, such as measles and the smallpox. Many believe this introduction quickly led to a plague, which ultimately wiped out ninety percent of the rather densely populated group in Mexico, and perhaps in the Inca empire. Europeans, therefore, came not only mounted on horses and with firearms, but were immune to diseases which had an impact even worse than that of the Black Death in Europe a century and a half earlier. This may have had enormous consequences in the ability of the Spaniards to make their conquest.

Lester Crocker: I was a professor specializing in the Enlightenment. My question is, perhaps, a leading one. It was suggested by Dr. Anshen's opening remarks, and Lord Thomas's insistence on the similarities between two cultures that were entirely disparate and separate and attributing these similarities to innate-ism. It is well-known that there was in Europe at that time, a well-developed theory of natural law, according to which universal values, however derived, were applicable to human conduct. This was, I think, Dr. Anshen's remark toward the end of her opening. Now, we all know, also, that the idea of innate-ism was refuted by Locke, that natural law was derided by Hume and other jurists, Blackstone, down through the nineteenth century and in the twentieth, Main in England, Oliver Wendell Holmes in the United States, and so forth. Are you suggesting to us that we ought to reconsider this opposition to natural law theory and feel that there is a justifiable, universal human value system, however violated in various circumstances, however differently interpreted, as Voltaire said, in different parts of the world?

DISCUSSION

John Archibald Wheeler: Surprise! In the world of science, the importance of a new discovery registers itself in the amount of surprise it occasions. Does a like principle hold in the world of human affairs? Lord Hugh Thomas and Professor Jorge Klor de Alva have given us a fascinating account of the cultural shock that Spaniards and Aztecs experienced as they encountered each other in war and peace. The clash of culture against culture left the world enriched. Having lived in Mexico and having worked there in a 400-year-old silver mine and having profited over later years from discussions of physics with Mexican colleagues, I am one of the many who is in love with Mexico, its color, its people and its dynamism. If you would understand another culture, it has been said, fight it. Or, if I may paraphrase Henry James, "To hate is to distrust. To distrust is to probe. To probe is to study. To study is to appreciate. To appreciate is to defend. To defend is to love." Fight it—or push against it—shoulder to shoulder. Commodore Matthew Perry, with his warships moored in Tokyo Bay, pushed the Shogun in 1853 and 1854 as Hernán Cortes pushed Montezuma in 1519. Japan had the strength to hold together. Mexico did not. How different Mexico and the Americas would look today if the Empire of Montezuma had had Japan's cohesion to stand against Cortes. Think of the world of today being dominated by Aztec motor cars, Aztec electronics and Aztec banking syndicates.

History, deriving its irresistible fascination from the age-old story of challenge and response, offers few instances of greater differences between colliding cultures than Tokyo Bay in 1853–54, and the events of 1519 related to us by Lord Hugh Thomas. Is there any chance that the future will bring us a still greater shock? After all, inspired not least by the example of Columbus, we have already entered the century of the exploration of space. There are billions of years ahead of us, and billions upon billions of potential living places on far away planets that await our landing. We cannot exclude the possibility of clash with a culture that will differ even more from ours than did the Mexico of 1519 or the Japan of 1853–1854. Who is to say how the encounter will turn out? What weapons will be brought to bear? What new organizational challenges will crop up? What will new ideas and novel disease germs do as they encounter hosts of untested resistance?

It was not foreordained how events would turn out when Cortes confronted Montezuma nor when Commodore Perry and his fleet challenged the Shogun. However the future encounter turns out, it will be a precious gain for our world if it brings us all a fraction of what Japan and Mexico have contributed to our ways of life and thought.

CONCLUSION

J. Jorge Klor de Alva: I don't think I'm going to touch the question on the brain because I do not know a thing about the brain. I will say in parentheses, however, that one of the philosophers who is being studied most by those working within the human sciences, who might consider themselves poststructuralists or postmodernists, is Kant, and more particularly, Kant's "What Is Enlightenment?" Therefore, I think it is wonderfully perceptive to have located Kant in the middle of this discussion. He is very much a part of the intellectual debates of the present; somewhere between Nietzsche and Kant we have much to resolve that is relevant to today's world. But that is all I am going to say about the brain!

However, having spent twenty years doing research on the Aztecs and studying sixteenth-century Mexico, I would like to make some very brief statements. With regard to Professor Schlesinger's comment, I believe it beyond question that if widespread diseases and the complex effects of the epidemics had not occurred, the Americas in general, especially from south of the area where the northern boundary of Mesoamerica is today to at least across the length of the Andes, would be very much like India is today. If diseases had not taken place, I would be speaking to you with a Nahuatl accent; but as you can hear, although I can speak in Nahuatl, mine is a Mexican not a Nahuatl accent. But in the absence of widespread epidemics, I could have been speaking to you with a Nahuatl accent because there would have been millions of people who would have continued their traditional ways in all those American areas, such as Mexico, that were densely populated for centuries before contact with the Europeans took place. These areas surely would have undergone some form of colonization and eventually, perhaps in the 1940s, the colonists would have been thrown out. And had this happened, the peoples and cultures would then not look as European as they do. Thus the world would certainly be very different from what it is today.

And with regard to cross-cultural morality, since "nice guys and dirty rats" are evenly distributed across all cultures—such that it leads me to think that this phenomenon is the mathematicians' and statisticians' source for the notion of random distribution—it is not useful to think of any side as monopolizing the moral high ground. So all that has been noted here is not a question of morals at all. But it is certainly a question about, for instance, the profound social and historical effects of the diseases brought by the Europeans. I have argued in a number of

CONCLUSION

forums that the Americas were never colonized as we understand the term today. I claim that the idea of colonization that is used today to describe the first three centuries after the European-Indian encounter is drawn primarily from late nineteenth- and early twentieth-centuries notions which have been applied retroactively to a time when the world was extremely different. In short, just as the cultural and social roles of diseases need to be rethought, there is much need to completely reconsider whether this sociopolitical category has any significance whatsoever to the reality of the time, especially for the non-Indians in the Americas.

I want to say a few more words specifically about the Aztecs. Those of us working in the area of what we call Nahuatl studies now know many things that could not have been known fifteen years ago, such as the likelihood that there are more documents in Nahuatl than in the whole of the Latin and Greek corpus. With these sources we can reconstruct Mesoamerican history today with the same finesse, through the same finely tuned perceptions, as we can for any place in Europe. In addition we now understand, as a consequence of this, that the Europeans who first arrived thought the same thing of the Nahuas as we; that is, that Cortes immediately realized, as did others, that they were face to face with a civilization that was every bit the equivalent of their own, perhaps not in some things, perhaps—I don't do art history—perhaps not in pottery, perhaps not in textiles, perhaps not in some things. I don't know how to debate these points of comparative art. But that in most other ways, in terms of medicine, social organization, et cetera, this civilization was very much like any other in Europe.

The Europeans themselves did not start seeing it otherwise until those stricken native lives started slipping through their hands. By the time that the later writings came to describe the Aztecs as pejorative "Indians," as opposed to the heretical but civilized Moors, by that time, the population of Mexico—to take but one relevant and notable example—had declined from perhaps twenty-five million to one million. By that time there were already hundreds of thousands of Spanish immigrants, thousands of enslaved Africans, and thousands upon thousands of growing numbers of hybrids or *castas*. Through depopulation the New World had become another world and, by that time, our impoverished idea of Indian came to take place. But that had not been the case at the moment of contact, not in central Mexico. Certainly it would have been a very different world today, there as here, had those diseases not taken place.

Hugh Thomas: Let me take, if I can, the last statement, which was extremely interesting, by Professor Klor de Alva. I think that what he said was important for two reasons: First, the change in perception between what the Spanish saw when they arrived in Mexico, and what they judged after the collapse of the population, which may have been as great as he indicated. This was a point which our friend over there also spoke about. I would like to know a little more about why it was that the Spanish in Mexico were able to resist these diseases more effectively. I see that the Spanish and the Mexicans had different immune systems. That is quite comprehensible; but, nevertheless, the diseases seem to have been ones which caused a lot of havoc in Europe as well. Smallpox did a lot of damage in Europe. Why was it that the Spanish in 1520, after their temporary retreat from Mexico, were able to ride through the country without being affected by the first big epidemic of smallpox which hit Mexico? It is a question which, I think, is a satisfactory one to leave unanswered, but it is a very interesting one.

There is just one thing, in this relation, on which I would like to challenge Professor Klor de Alva. The first epidemic was 1520. The great destruction of the Caribbean was before that. It is true that the Mexican population was immensely reduced as a result of disease, yet, there was a Mexican-Indian population still surviving in the seventeenth and eighteenth centuries. But that is not the case in the rest of the Caribbean where an indigenous Indian population, whose size is disputed but which may have been as large as two million, disappeared almost completely between 1492 and 1518–19. The smallpox epidemic, which hit Mexico in 1520, hit Santo Domingo (Hispaniola) in 1518–1519. But it didn't really have much effect since the population, by that time, was almost destroyed by overwork, by lack of cultural identification with the conquerors, and with a sense of complete alienation as a result of the death of the old society.

I was very interested by what Professor Klor de Alva said about Mexico and South America in general looking like India had it not been for these diseases. It is an important point to appreciate, though, and I think you will agree with it, that Mexico, has something in common with India, even now, in that it is a country of many peoples who continue to accept a common, overall political structure.

CONCLUSION

I am going to come now to other points that emerged in the discussion. Reference has been made to the destruction of the Caribbean society, I wasn't quite sure whether he meant Mexico, or he meant the Caribbean. I think, actually, that the Caribbean before the Spanish got there was relatively peaceful. It is true I think that the Caribs were fighting their way up like pirates throughout the eastern Caribbean islands and bringing havoc and possible cannibalism to those islands. But the Taino in Cuba and in Hispaniola does not seem to be in any way bellicose. Therefore, the picture which Columbia took back on his first voyage, but not on his other voyages—if, indeed, he wrote the diary, which he is supposed to have written, giving an idyllic picture of the Caribbean—was closer to reality than might be supposed. The picture of Mexico was one of violence in which an unpopular imperial regime was maintained by military power, and that was the reason for the overthrow of the system eventually.

Professor Kristeller challenged me on two points. First, that there is a good deal of gold and silver and other Mexican artifacts left. There is not very much gold and silver left. In fact, there wasn't much silver anyway. There wasn't a silver industry of the scale that there was a gold one, but most of the Aztec gold has certainly been lost. The great gold wheel, which Dürer saw in Brussels, was melted down. Heaven knows where it went. It is surprising that it was melted down, since it was admired, at the time, by everyone who saw it, not only Dürer, but Peter Martir, Las Casas, and others who all recalled having seen it. Pottery is a question of judgment. I said that the achievement of Mayan and Aztec pottery was equivalent to that of Europeans. Where I think I must concede, where I think I may have misled the audience, is in relation to mathematics. I meant to say that the Mexican and Meso-American knowledge of the calendar was superior. I didn't mean to leave the impression that that applied to mathematics in general.

My notes on Professor Wheeler's intervention are not as clear a they should be. I think that his question was: "Would it matter if there had been no people in the Americas when Columbus and Cortes arrived?" Well, there was an American Indian population for several thousand years. There were only two or three substantial settled peoples: the Mexicans, the Incas, and those who lived in other parts of what is now referred to as Meso-America. The rest were primarily nomadic. I have no doubt that the picture which Professor Klor de Alva gave of the society which the Aztecs had established was as superior as that which he implied, and that which the Spanish describe. He gave a good picture of that, and it is correct that it was observed as such at the time. It was not realized by those to whom Cortes was writing that was what it was, but it was the case.

The question raised as to whether I am suggesting that we should reconsider innate-ism is an extremely interesting one. I raised that, since, as I say, there are so many similarities in the conduct of affairs by the Mexicans that you cannot deny that this is a civilization which had, as Cortes referred to, "order and harmony." I don't necessarily think that it should be regarded as innate-ism, but I certainly would say that once a settled community has taken shape, once priests, monarchs, class structure, taxes, commerce are equally established, then there are certain predictable characteristics which I felt I could use the word "innate" to describe.

I think that the main point which I made was not really that which Arthur Schlesinger indicated I had, namely, that here were so many similarities. That was a very important subsidiary point. My main point is that the discovery of America, as commemorated by 1992, recalling 1492, is somewhat misplaced, despite the great work which is going on to commemorate it, because of the fact that Columbus did not discover the great centers of American culture and civilization such as Mexico and Peru. These places were the heart of Old America.

When Diego Rivera came to New York in 1926, he said, specifically to his United States hosts, to their discomfiture, "What you don't seem to realize is that we Americans have antiquities in Mexico, and I am commemorating them as best I can."

The United States, particularly the last generation, has looked toward Europe, looked toward the world, much more than toward its neighbors, less than it should have done. I suspect that one of the great benefits of the 1992 celebration will be to insist on appropriate recognition of the importance of Latin American, and particularly Mexican and Peruvian society in the history of the Americas. Perhaps that will, therefore, make up for the possible misplaced emphasis on Columbus's own role and the events immediately following the first voyage of 1492.

I hope that Dr. Anshen feels that this most interesting

CONCLUSION

and important discussion has seemed worthy of her great energy and investment of time. She has done a wonderful thing to inspire this series of lectures. I notice that I am the only historian in this first group of lectures, and it is a great privilege to have fulfilled that position.

BIOGRAPHICAL NOTES

RUTH NANDA ANSHEN, PH.D., Fellow of the Royal Society of Arts of London, founded, plans, and edits several distinguished series of books, including World Perspectives, Religious Perspectives, Credo Perspectives, Perspectives in Humanism, the Science of Culture Series, the Tree of Life Series, and Convergence. She has exerted remarkable influence through her worldwide lectures, her writings, her ability to attract a most important group of contributors to these series, underlying the unitary principle of all reality, and particularly through her close association with many of the great scientists and thinkers of this century, from Whitehead, Einstein, Bohr, and Heisenberg to Rabi, Tillich, Chomsky, and Wheeler. Dr. Anshen's book *The Reality of the Devil: Evil in Man*, a study in the phenomenology of evil, demonstrates the interrelationship between good and evil. She is also the author of *Anatomy of Evil* and *Biography of an Idea*, and her volume *Morals Equals Manners* was published in February 1992. Dr. Anshen is a member of the American Philosophical Association, the History of Science Society, the International Philosophical Society, and the Metaphysical Society of America.

Lecture Hugh Thomas, Lord Thomas of Swynnerton

HUGH THOMAS, whose father was of Welsh origin, was educated at Sherborne, Queens College, Cambridge, and the Sorbonne. He had a distinguished career in the Foreign Office, and in the years from 1966 to 1976 was Professor of History at the University of Reading. Between 1979 and 1990 he was chairman of the Center for Policy Studies, an institute for political research. In 1981 he was made a life peer, and since then he has spoken on international and educational questions in the House of Lords. In 1957 he published his first novel, *The World's Game*, followed in 1961 by *The Spanish Civil War*, republished many times and in many languages. His history of Cuba—*Cuba, or the Pursuit of Freedom*—was published in 1971; the second part was republished in 1988 as *The Cuban Revolution*. Other works have included a study of the Suez Crisis entitled *The Suez Affair*, *Goya and The Third of May 1808*, *John Strachey* (a biography), *An Unfinished History of the World*, and *Armed Truce*, a study of the origins of the Cold War. Hugh Thomas recently completed a study of contemporary Mexico for the Twentieth Century Foundation in New York (provisionally entitled *The Mexican Labyrinth*). He is currently engaged in a reexamination of the issues involved in the Spanish Conquest of Mexico. In recent years he has published two novels, *Havannah* (1984) and *Klara* (1988). On European questions, he published *Europe, the Radical Challenge* (1973), brought up to date in another essay of persuasion, *Ever Closer Union*, published in January 1991.

Discussion Leader J. Jorge Klor de Alva, Professor of Anthropology, Princeton University

Professor KLOR DE ALVA was born in Mexico City. His higher education was at the University of California (both at Berkeley and Santa Cruz), and he is now a citizen of the United States. He has taught throughout this country in anthropology, Mesoamerican studies, and Latin American studies. His many publications have dealt with contemporary interpretation of the New World, Aztec and Nahua culture, and Mexican philosophy, personality, language, and justice. He is a member of the coordinating committees or commissions of several institutes, exhibitions, and panels for the Quincentennial celebrations in Spain in 1992; and he is the Head Curator responsible for the anthropology/history section of building number one of the Spanish government's "Pavilion of the Discoveries" at Expo-92 in Seville.

Discussants
Professor Arthur Schlesinger, Jr.
Albert Schweitzer Professor in the Humanities
Graduate School, City University of New York

BIOGRAPHICAL NOTES

Dr. Marvin Ruderman
Centennial Professor of Physics,
Columbia University

Dr. James H. Schwartz
Scientist and Scholar in Neuro-Biology,
College of Physicians and Surgeons,
Columbia University Presbyterian Center

Paul Oscar Kristeller
Woodbridge Professor Emeritus of Philosophy,
Columbia University

Professor John Archibald Wheeler
Joseph Henry Professor of Physics Emeritus,
Princeton University

Lester Crocker
Professor of Eighteenth Century Philosophy,
Dean of the Humanities Division,
University of Virginia